NATIONAL GEOGRAPHIC

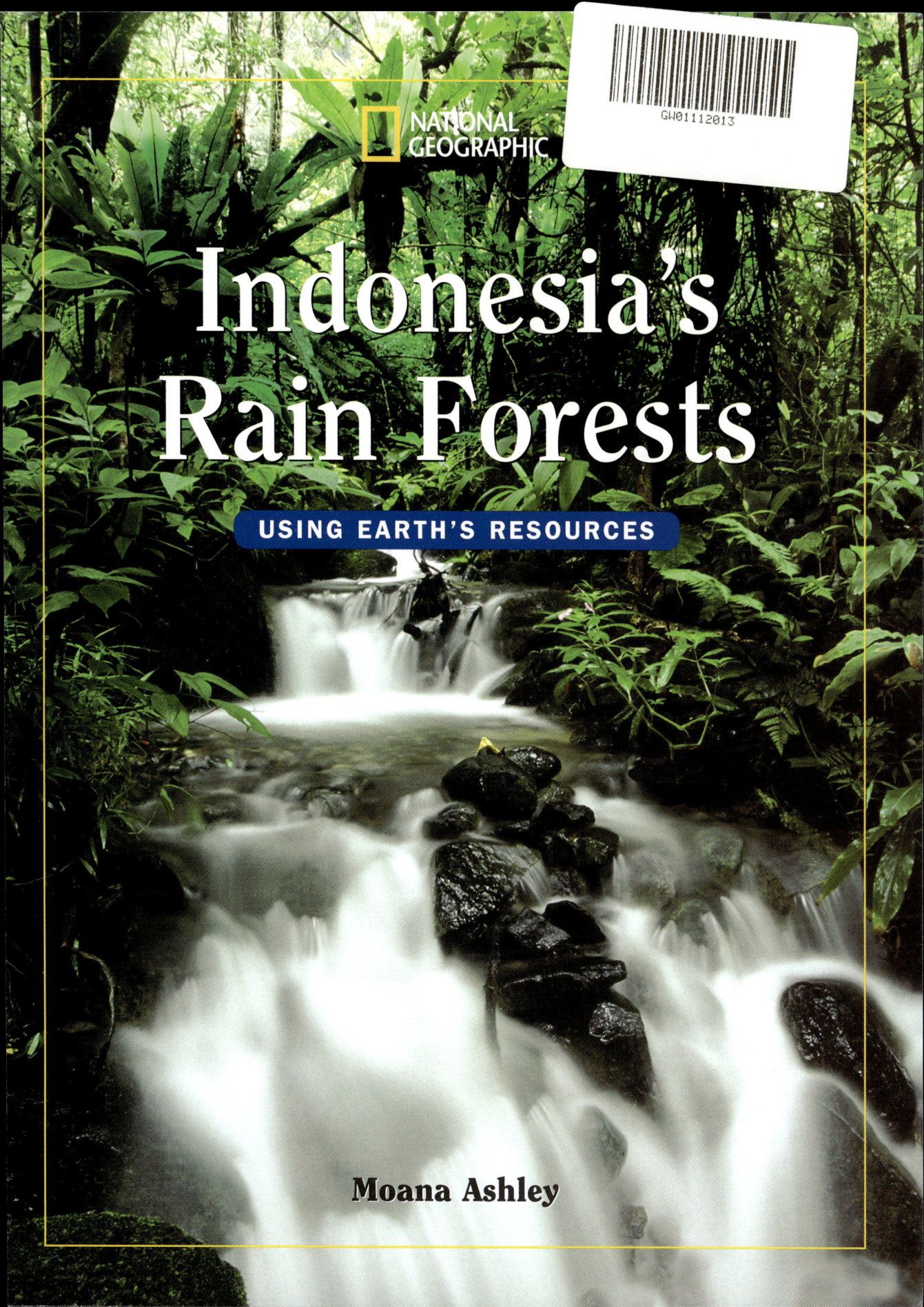

Indonesia's Rain Forests

USING EARTH'S RESOURCES

Moana Ashley

PICTURE CREDITS
Cover: ferns growing in a cloud forest © Wayne Lawler; Ecoscene/
Corbis/Tranz; logging trucks, Corbis.

page 1 © Gavriel Jecan/Corbis/Tranz; page 4 (bottom left) ©
Wayne Lawler; Ecoscene/Corbis/Tranz; page 4 (bottom right) ©
Wolfgang Kaehler/Corbis/Tranz; page 5 (top)
© Reinhard Eisele/Corbis/Tranz; page 5 (bottom left), Photodisc;
page 5 (bottom right) © Jim Zuckerman/Corbis/Tranz; page 6,
Digital Vision; page 8 © Wayne Lawler; Ecoscene/Corbis/Tranz;
page 9 (left), Digital Vision; page 9 (right), Photodisc; page 11
© Lindsay Hebberd/Corbis/Tranz; page 12 © Tony Arruza/Corbis/
Tranz; page 13 © Dean Conger/Corbis/Tranz; page 15 © Theo
Allofs/Corbis/Tranz; page 16 © Lester Lefkowitz/Corbis/Tranz;
page 21 © Wayne Lawler; Ecoscene/Corbis/Tranz; page 22
© Konrad Wothe/Minden Pictures/Stock Image Group; page 23
© Martin Harvey/Corbis/Tranz; page 24 © Viviane Moos/Corbis/
Tranz; page 25 © Gavriel Jecan/Corbis/Tranz; page 26 © Reinhard
Eisele/Corbis/Tranz; page 29, Brand X Pictures.

Produced through the worldwide resources of the National
Geographic Society, John M. Fahey, Jr., President and Chief
Executive Officer; Gilbert M. Grosvenor, Chairman of the Board.

PREPARED BY NATIONAL GEOGRAPHIC SCHOOL PUBLISHING
Sheron Long, Chief Executive Officer; Samuel Gesumaria,
President; Steve Mico, Executive Vice President and Publisher;
Francis Downey, Editor in Chief; Richard Easby, Editorial Manager;
Margaret Sidlosky, Director of Design and Illustrations; Jim Hiscott,
Design Manager; Cynthia Olson and Ruth Ann Thompson, Art
Directors; Matt Wascavage, Director of Publishing Services; Lisa
Pergolizzi, Production Manager.

MANUFACTURING AND QUALITY CONTROL
Christopher A. Liedel, Chief Financial Officer; Phillip L. Schlosser,
Vice President; Clifton M. Brown III, Director.

EDITOR
Mary Anne Wengel

PROGRAMME CONSULTANTS
Dr. Shirley V. Dickson, National Literacy Consultant; James A.
Shymansky, E. Desmond Lee Professor of Science Education,
University of Missouri-St Louis.

Copyright © 2007 Macmillan Education Australia.

First published in 2007 in Great Britain by Kingscourt/McGraw-Hill
publishers.

McGraw-Hill International (UK) Limited
McGraw-Hill House
Shoppenhangers Road, Maidenhead
Berkshire, SL6 2QL

www.kingscourt.co.uk

The materials in this publication may be photocopied for use
only within the purchasing organisation. Otherwise, all rights
reserved and no part of the publication may be reproduced,
stored in a retrieval system or transmitted, in any form, or by
any means, electronic, mechanical, photocopying, recording or
otherwise, without prior permission of the publishers. National
Geographic, National Geographic Explorer, and the Yellow Border
are trademarks of the National Geographic Society.

ISBN–13: 978-1-4202-1792-6

Printed in Hong Kong.

2011 2010 2009 2008 2007
1 2 3 4 5 6 7 8 9 10 11 12 13 14 15

Contents

💡 Using Earth's Resources 4

Rain Forest Resources 6

💡 Think About the Key Concepts 17

Visual Literacy
Resource Map 18

Genre Study
Problem-Solution Article 20

Saving the Rain Forests in Indonesia 21

💡 Apply the Key Concepts 27

Research and Write
Write Your Own Problem-Solution Article 28

Glossary 31

Index 32

Using Earth's Resources

Nature provides people with many useful things. Air, water, plants, animals, minerals, and fuels all come from nature. Things that come from nature are called natural resources. Natural resources are found everywhere on Earth. They are found in the rain forests of Indonesia, the ocean region of Greenland, the deserts of Australia, and the mountains of Peru.

Key Concepts

1. Earth provides many natural resources that people can use.
2. Different resources are useful to people in different ways.
3. Conservation and recycling can help save resources.

Four Resource-Rich Regions

Tropical Rain Forests

The trees in Indonesia's rain forests have many important uses.

Oceans

The oceans around Greenland teem with marine animals.

In this book you will learn about the resources found in Indonesia's tropical rain forests.

Deserts

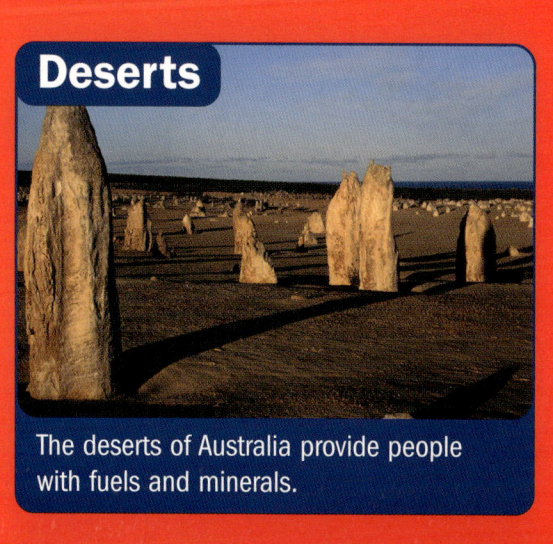

The deserts of Australia provide people with fuels and minerals.

Mountains

The mountains of Peru offer a wealth of useful trees and minerals.

Rain Forest Resources

Imagine walking through a tropical rain forest. What do you see? You see tall trees and thick shrubs. Colorful flowers are all around. In fact, more than half the world's plant species live in tropical rain forests. Much of the country of Indonesia is covered with tropical rain forests.

Tropical Rain Forests

Tropical rain forests grow in hot, wet places. The temperature is warm or hot all year. Plants and trees in tropical rain forests need a large amount of rain. They need at least 198 centimeters (78 inches) of rain a year.

Tropical rain forest in Indonesia

The Tropical Rain Forests of Indonesia

Indonesia is a country in Asia. It is made up of more than 17,500 islands. The **climate** of Indonesia is warm and wet. About half of Indonesia is covered in rain forests. Millions of trees and other plants grow in these forests.

Look at the map. It shows where Indonesia's tropical rain forests are located.

Indonesia's Rain Forests

Key: Rain forest

Key Concept 1 Earth provides many natural resources that people can use.

Natural Resources

People get many **natural resources** from rain forests. Natural resources are things found in nature that people can use. Most things that people make, wear, or eat start out as natural resources.

natural resources: materials that are found in nature and are useful to people

There are many kinds of natural resources. Trees, plants, air, and water are examples of natural resources. They are all things found in nature. They are all things used by people.

Wood from Indonesia's rain forests is a natural resource.

Resources from Indonesia's Rain Forests

Trees are one of the most important natural resources from a rain forest. They provide us with many useful things. Some trees provide food, such as fruits and nuts. Other trees provide wood to use for building. Wood is used to build furniture and boats. Wood is also used to make paper.

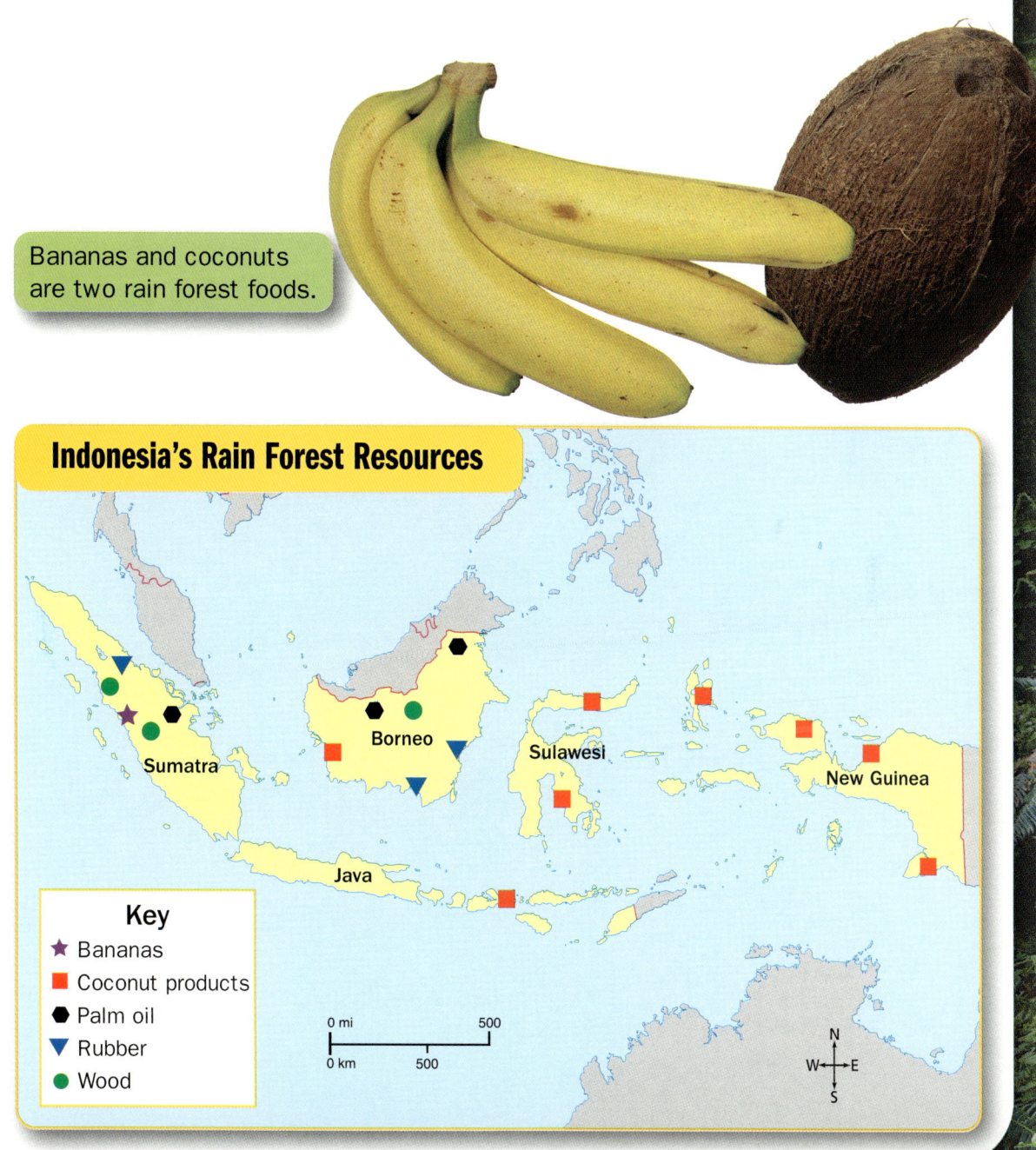

Bananas and coconuts are two rain forest foods.

Indonesia's Rain Forest Resources

Key
- ★ Bananas
- ■ Coconut products
- ⬢ Palm oil
- ▼ Rubber
- ● Wood

9

Rain Forests and the Oxygen Cycle

Trees play a part in the oxygen cycle. Rain forests turn carbon dioxide into oxygen. People and animals breathe the oxygen. Then they breathe out carbon dioxide, and the cycle starts again.

Rain forests produce about 50 percent of Earth's oxygen. Without rain forests, Earth may not get the oxygen it needs.

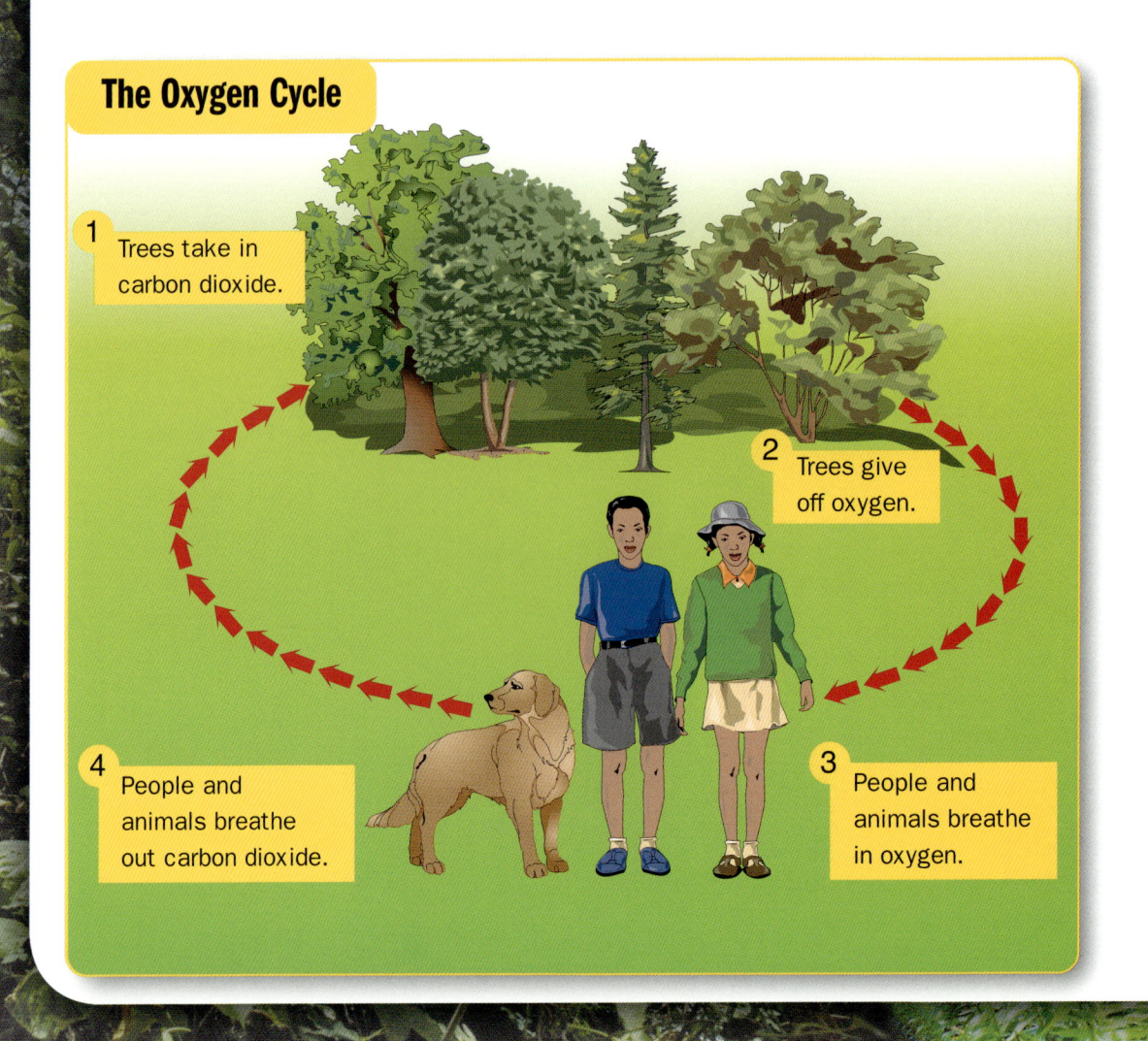

The Oxygen Cycle

1. Trees take in carbon dioxide.
2. Trees give off oxygen.
3. People and animals breathe in oxygen.
4. People and animals breathe out carbon dioxide.

Key Concept 2 Different resources are useful to people in different ways.

How Rain Forest Trees Are Used

Indonesia's rain forests have many different types of trees. Each type of tree has **properties**, or qualities, that make it different from other trees. People use the trees to make different products.

Some of the wood from the Indonesian rain forest is used to make furniture, such as this crib.

Hardwood Trees

Some of the tallest rain forest trees are hardwood trees. They include teak and ironwood trees. Hardwood is strong and heavy. Hardwood does not absorb water easily. These properties make hardwood good for making furniture and boats.

Hardwood trees are also used to make paper. The **fibers** that make up hardwoods are short. These short fibers are good for making paper that is smooth or soft.

A carpenter lays teak decking on a ship.

Palm Trees

The rain forests of Indonesia have many types of palm trees. Some palm trees, such as coconut trees, give people food. Other palm trees, such as rattan trees, have leaves with strong stems. People use the stems to make baskets and furniture. Most palm trees also contain oil. People use the oil for cooking. They also use the oil for making soap and candles.

Cinchona Trees

Cinchona (sihn-koh-nuh) trees also grow in the rain forests of Indonesia. People use the bark of the cinchona to make quinine. Quinine is a medicine used to treat **malaria**. Malaria is a common disease in tropical places. Most of the quinine used today comes from Indonesia.

Indonesian workers drying coconuts in the sun

Key Concept 3 Conservation and recycling can help save resources.

Using Earth's Resources Wisely

There are two kinds of resources on Earth. The first kind is **renewable** resources. These resources get replaced by nature. Trees and animals are renewable resources. The other kind is **nonrenewable** resources. These resources, such as metals, do not get replaced. One day, they will run out.

People have to take care of Earth's resources. Some nonrenewable resources are running out. Some renewable resources are being used faster than Earth can replace them. People need to use Earth's resources carefully. If they are used wisely, they will be there for future use.

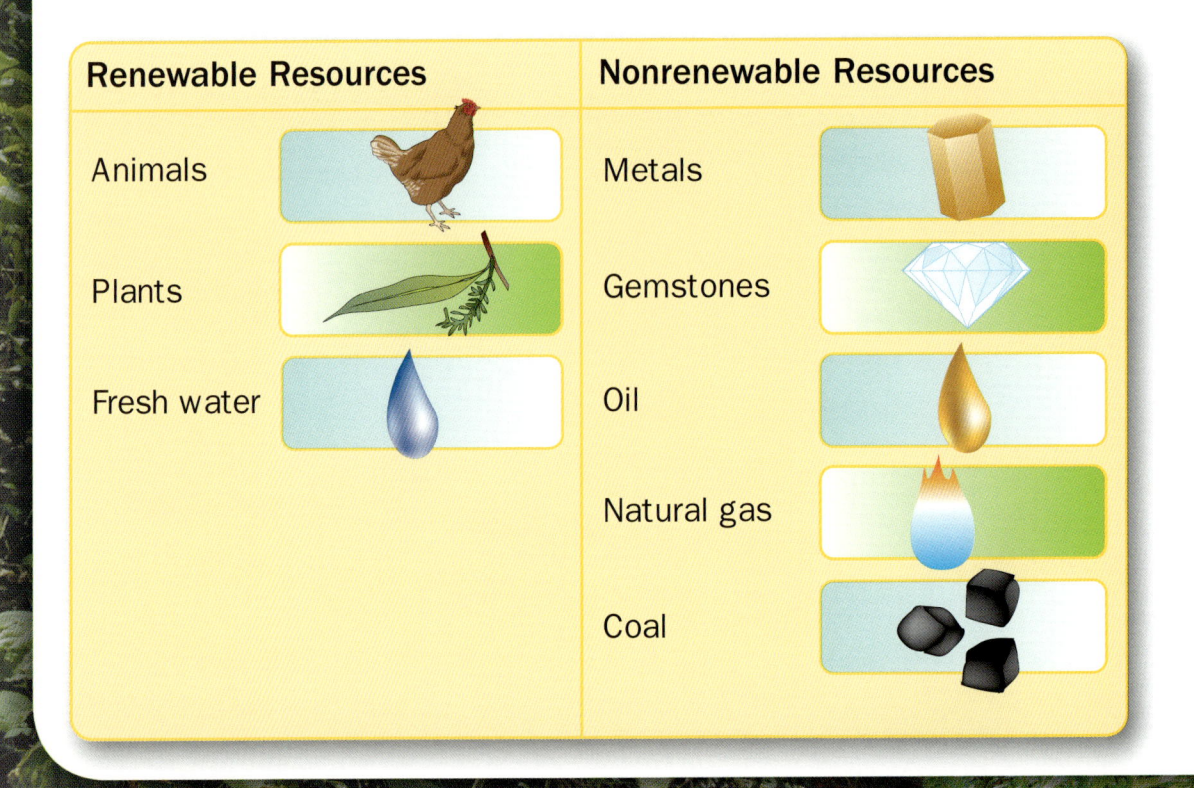

Renewable Resources		Nonrenewable Resources	
Animals		Metals	
Plants		Gemstones	
Fresh water		Oil	
		Natural gas	
		Coal	

Conservation

Conservation is one way people can help save Earth's resources. Conservation is the careful use of a resource.

> **conservation**
> protection and careful use of natural resources

Indonesia's rain forests have begun to disappear. People have cut down trees faster than they can grow back. The Indonesian government is trying to help conserve the rain forests. The government has made laws to protect the forests.

People around the world can also help conserve the rain forest. People can use less paper. They can buy fewer things made from rain forest wood. If people do these things, maybe fewer trees will be cut down.

Tanjung Puting National Park in Indonesia protects trees and wildlife, such as these orangutans.

Recycling

Another way to conserve resources is by **recycling**. To recycle is to turn used products into new products.

> **recycling**
> turning used material into new products

Paper is one product that can be recycled. Old, used paper is broken down and made into new paper. This means that fewer trees need to be cut down to make new paper.

Many of the trees in Indonesia's rain forests get made into paper. By recycling paper, people can help save forests.

Paper is recycled at a recycling center.

Think About the Key Concepts

Think about what you read. Think about the maps and diagrams. Use these to answer the questions. Share what you think with others.

1. Name two or more resources from the country you read about in this book.

2. Name at least three ways the natural resources discussed in this book are used.

3. Explain the difference between a renewable resource and a nonrenewable resource.

4. Give at least two examples of how people can conserve Earth's resources.

VISUAL LITERACY

Resource Map

A resource map shows you the natural resources found in an area.
Resource maps often use symbols to show where the different kinds of resources are found.

Resource maps can show different kinds of resources.
Look back at the resource map on page 9. It shows where rain forest resources are found in Indonesia. The map on page 19 is also a resource map. It shows where the main food resources are grown or farmed around the world.

How to Read a Resource Map

1. **Read the title.**
   The title tells you which type of resource will be shown on the map.
2. **Read the key.**
   The key tells you what the different symbols represent.
3. **Study the map.**
   Find the symbols on the map to see which resources are found in which areas.

Main World Food Resources

Key

- ★ Barley
- ● Cattle
- ● Citrus fruit
- ● Coffee
- ✚ Corn
- ● Grapes
- ✚ Oats
- ● Pigs
- ★ Potatoes
- ▲ Poultry
- ▼ Rice
- ✚ Sheep
- ★ Soybeans
- ■ Sugarcane
- ◆ Tea
- ✚ Wheat

What's on the Map?

Read the map by following the directions on page 18. Then use the map to answer the following questions. What are the main crops grown in South America? On which continents are cattle raised for food? What foods are produced near the area where you live?

GENRE STUDY

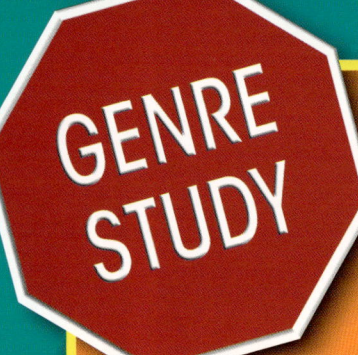

Problem-Solution Article

A problem-solution article describes a problem and gives possible solutions to the problem. The problem-solution article beginning on page 21 describes the problem of loss of forests in Indonesia.

A problem-solution article usually contains the following:

The Introduction
The introduction outlines the problem.

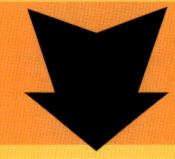

The Problem
The first body paragraphs explain how the problem came about.

The Solutions
The next body paragraphs give some possible solutions to the problem.

Saving the Rain Forests in Indonesia

*The **title** tells you the topic of the article.*

The rain forests in Indonesia are an important resource. But this resource is facing a problem. More than 2 million hectares (4.94 million acres) of rain forest are destroyed each year. This is an area about the size of the state of New Jersey.

*The **introduction** outlines the problem.*

Some trees are cut down for wood. Other trees are burned to clear land. The cleared land is used for growing crops or mining for minerals.

***Photographs** support the facts in the text.*

Many areas that were once forest in Indonesia have been cleared.

The Problem: Loss of Forests

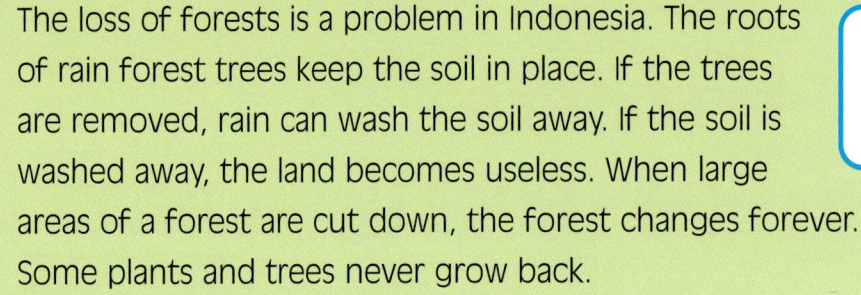

The loss of forests is a problem in Indonesia. The roots of rain forest trees keep the soil in place. If the trees are removed, rain can wash the soil away. If the soil is washed away, the land becomes useless. When large areas of a forest are cut down, the forest changes forever. Some plants and trees never grow back.

> The first body paragraphs explain how the **problem** came about.

When rain forests are destroyed, many animals die. The animals lose their homes. They also lose their source of food. Some animals in Indonesia are at risk of dying out. The orangutan is one animal at risk. In the last 20 years, about 80 percent of orangutans' habitat has been lost.

Logging

Logging is the main cause of the loss of forests. Logging is the cutting down of trees for their wood. Wood from rain forest trees is used for making furniture. It is also used for making paper.

The orangutan is just one of many animals affected by the destruction of Indonesia's forests.

This logger has cut down a large rain forest tree in Indonesia.

Farming

Farming also destroys Indonesia's rain forests. Many farmers burn forests to clear land for farming. Some farmers use the land to grow crops. Other farmers use the land to keep farm animals. Large areas of rain forest have been burned to make way for farms.

Mining

People also cut down the rain forest for mining. Mining is digging into the ground to find minerals. Materials such as copper, gold, tin, coal, and oil are mined in Indonesia.

The Solutions

Several things might solve the problem of the loss of forests in Indonesia. These include passing strict laws, replanting forests, and practicing conservation.

> The next body paragraphs give some possible **solutions** to the problem.

Strict Laws

One solution is to create strict laws against cutting down rain forest trees. The government of Indonesia has already made many laws to protect rain forests. Some of these laws stop people from mining in forest areas. Other laws stop the clearing of forests for farming.

This area was once rain forest. Laws can make clearing rain forests illegal.

Mount Gede National Park in Indonesia is protected by law from logging and mining.

In 2001, the government made a law against selling timber from hardwood trees. One kind of hardwood tree, the ramin tree, is valuable for making furniture and other products. If people obey these laws, Indonesia's rain forests can be saved.

Planting New Trees

Another way to solve the problem is to plant new trees. These new trees are planted where the forest has been cut down. About 13.2 million hectares (32.6 million acres) of land where forest has been destroyed are being replanted in Indonesia. This area of land is just bigger than the state of Pennsylvania.

Conservation

Conservation is also a way to help save Indonesia's rain forests. People can choose not to buy goods made from rain forest trees. Then, perhaps, fewer trees would be cut down.

Teaching Indonesian people how to conserve the rain forests can also help. People can make a living from the rain forests without cutting down trees. They can get goods such as nuts, fruits, and herbs from the forests. If rain forests are looked after, their resources could last forever.

A man collects coconuts from a rain forest in Indonesia.

Apply the Key Concepts

Key Concept 1 Earth provides many natural resources that people can use.

Activity Write a list of four things that you use every day, such as kinds of food or clothing. Then write down the natural resources that these things come from. For example, they might come from plants or animals.

> 1. Wool sweater: wool comes from sheep
> 2. Apples: grow on trees
> 3.

Key Concept 2 Different resources are useful to people in different ways.

Activity Create a chart with three columns. In the first column, name some resources found in Indonesia's rain forests. In the second column, name the special properties of each natural resource. In the third column, name the ways people use each natural resource.

Resource	Properties	Uses

Key Concept 3 Conservation and recycling can help save resources.

Activity Write a short letter to a conservation group. Give two reasons why you think Indonesia's rain forests should be conserved. Give one suggestion for how people can help conserve the rain forests.

> To whom it may concern:
> _____
> _____
> _____
> _____

RESEARCH AND WRITE

Write Your Own Problem-Solution Article

You have read the problem-solution article about loss of rain forests in Indonesia. Now you can write your own problem-solution article.

1. Study the Model

Look back at pages 21–26. Read the labels to find the important features of a problem-solution article. What information is presented in the introduction section of the article? What information is presented in *The Problem* section of the article? What information is presented in *The Solutions* section of the article?

Writing a Problem-Solution Article

- Choose a topic related to conservation. The topic must have a problem and possible solutions.
- Write an introduction explaining what needs to be conserved.
- Write several body paragraphs describing the problem.
- Write several more paragraphs giving some solutions to the problem.

2. Choose Your Topic

Now you can choose your topic. Your topic will be a conservation issue. It must involve a problem for which there are possible solutions. You may choose an animal that is at risk of dying out. You may choose an area where the natural environment is at risk. You may already know of a conservation cause that you would like to research. Otherwise, look on the Internet and through books and magazines to get some ideas.

3. Research Your Topic

Write down notes on what you already know about your topic. Organize them into columns labeled "Problem" and "Solution." Then think about what else you will need to find out. Remember that you will need to discuss the conservation problem in the first section. In the second section, you will need to present some possible solutions to the problem.

Topic: Giant Pandas

Problem	Solution
Habitat destruction	Protect the bamboo forests

Make a list of questions. Use this list to guide your research. Then look through books and magazines. Go on the Internet. Take notes on what you find out and add them to your chart. Make copies of pictures you may want to use.

4. Write a Draft

Now you can write a draft of your article. Look back at the article on pages 21–26. Use it as a model for writing your article.

5. Revise and Edit

Read your draft. Check to see that it is well organized. Keep your research nearby so you can check that all the facts are correct. Look for any words that are misspelled. Make sure that each sentence starts with a capital letter.

SHARING YOUR WORK

Create a Conservation Poster

Now you can share your work. You can design a poster about your conservation cause. Then you can share your poster with the rest of the class.

How to Make a Poster

1. **Think of a slogan.**
   A slogan is a catchy phrase. It sums up your conservation goal, for example, "Save the Pandas." Write your slogan in big letters on your poster paper.

2. **Include a strong photograph or illustration.**
   Use a copy of a photograph you found during your research. Or draw an illustration on your poster. The photograph or illustration should show the animal or natural environment that you want to conserve.

3. **Write some information about the cause.**
   Write a short paragraph about your animal or natural environment. Tell why it needs to be conserved. Give important facts. For example, you could write the number of pandas alive today compared to 50 years ago. Keep your sentences short and to the point.

4. **Share your work.**
   Hang all the class posters on the classroom wall. As a class, walk around the room and read each other's posters. Be prepared to answer any questions your classmates may have about your conservation cause.

Glossary

climate – the general weather conditions of a certain area

conservation – protection and careful use of natural resources

fibers – fine, threadlike particles that make up plants

malaria – a tropical disease that causes high fever and sometimes death

natural resources – materials that are found in nature and are useful to people

nonrenewable – not able to be replaced once it is used

properties – special features or qualities

recycling – turning used material into new products

renewable – able to be replaced by nature once it is used

Index

food 9, 13

natural resources 4, 8–9, 15

nonrenewable resources 14

oxygen cycle 10

paper 9, 12, 15–16

quinine 13

renewable resources 14

wood 8–9, 11, 15